love comes

An Advent Study Course

TONY CASTLE

Kevin Mayhew

First published in 1998 by
KEVIN MAYHEW LTD
Rattlesden
Bury St Edmunds
Suffolk IP30 0SZ

0 1 2 3 4 5 6 7 8 9

ISBN 1 84003 232 4
Catalogue No. 1500219

Cover design by Angela Staley
Typesetting by Louise Selfe
Printed in Great Britain

Contents

Dedicated to
The Reverend Brian Shannon
and his wife Alison
on their retirement

Foreword

Advent is an important and popular season of the Christian calendar. While practical aids to the celebration of the season – Advent calendars, Advent candles, wreaths and the like – abound, there is little help available for those who wish to explore the deeper spiritual meaning and purpose of the season.

While this book is primarily intended for group work, it can equally be used for individual and private preparation for Christmas. The material might also be adapted for use in the school assembly.

Each of the five chapters, one for each of the five weeks preceding Christmas, is arranged for use in the following way. Each participant reads the chapter before meeting with the group. When all are gathered, and after an introductory prayer, the group leader, or one of the group, reads out the *Summary*. This can be followed by the reading of the *Bible reading* for the week. The group leader then leads the discussion using the *Points* provided; there is space for making notes if desired. The meeting closes with the *Prayer*. The participants might be invited to use the prayer during the following week.

In putting this simple course together there has been a problem. Advent consists of *four* weeks but there are *three* 'Comings' of Christ identified by the Church in the Liturgy for Advent. The readings for the First Sunday of Advent speak of Christ coming one day as Judge. The Second and Third Sundays refer to John the Baptist and his introduction of Jesus, who comes as Messiah and Teacher. The Fourth Sunday of Advent focuses our attention on Mary of Nazareth as she is prepared for the coming of the Messiah as a helpless baby.

Hence the Second and Third Sundays both cover the same 'Coming', Jesus as the Messiah, our teacher and guide in life.

Ready for love

The meaning of Advent

I had just finished the story of how Mr Goldfinch, my grand-mother's milkman, had gone to prison, for watering down the milk he sold; (it was a lesson to help the class, 9C, understand that the Prophet Amos would have problems of injustice to sort out today) when Sheila, our kindly school secretary, appeared at the door of room E3 looking very serious. She drew me aside and said, 'Your mother is in intensive care at Buckland Hospital. I will look after things here. Go.'

As fast as I could I got home and immediately rang the hospital. I had heard from my brother Peter who lived close to my parents in Dover, the previous evening. He told me that Mum had had 'a bit of a turn', but had reassured me that there was nothing to worry about. This telephone conversation confirmed that my mother had suffered a massive stroke and was on a life support machine. I said 'I'll come immediately.' Even with good travelling conditions I knew that it would take me almost two hours and it did. And I was too late!

When someone we love is in trouble or in danger we do not need persuading to go to help them; we say 'I'll come'; and we go. There was a distinct difference between the two-hour-journey and the arrival. I lived in desperate hope as I travelled but when I arrived the hope turned to grief.

In this coming year I have a special birthday, one of those milestones that end in 0. It is still months away, but I am conscious of it coming. I do not expect my family to start celebrating until the day actually arrives. There is a distinct difference between an event or person 'coming' and their actual arrival. You cannot be waiting while the person is coming and, at the same time, celebrating their arrival. Yet that is exactly what happens every year in the weeks preceding 25 December!

The two Christmasses

In modern Britain there are two distinct celebrations of Christmas; the secular one of the consumer and the shops, and the religious one of the Christian. The word *Christmas* comes from the words *Mass of Christ's birth* gradually rendered, over time, into *Christ's Mass* and finally, because we are so lazy in our speech, *Christmas.*

This did not escape the attention of the Puritans of the seventeenth century who declared that Christmas was a Popish (their term for Catholic) festival and so should be banned; which, in 1647 and for thirteen years thereafter, it was!

Most people are under the impression that the birth of Christ has been celebrated by Christians from the beginning, but this is not so. The first recorded Mass to celebrate Christ's birth was in Rome, a little before AD 354. That year a certain Philocalus records, for the first time, a list of Christian festivals that begins with the winter solstice on 25 December and Christmas celebrated that day. As no one actually knew on which day Jesus was born, this seemed as good as any. Speculation among theologians and writers as to the actual date had gone on for some one hundred years before, with a wide range of dates proposed. For a while St Clement of Alexandria's suggestion that it should be 20 May was popular, but eventually the Church chose the date of the pagan festival of light, *Natalis Soli Invicti.* (the birthday of the sun). There was a certain logic in this since Christ was coming into the world as the Light of the world; as the 'Sun of Righteousness'. Gradually, as the years passed, the new Christian festival spread, from Rome, throughout Western Europe. (It would be very interesting to know when and how it was first celebrated in Britain; but no records of this appear to exist.)

The story goes that, in the early 1940s, a private member's bill was put before Parliament by a certain Mr Massey MP, proposing that, as most people in Britain did not go to church on Christmas Day or recall the birth of Christ, the festival should be re-named *Yuletide*. This, he argued, would return the winter festival to its original roots. Mr Massey was well-known as an outspoken agnostic and hostile critic of the Church. The debate was lively and an MP, well-known for his adherence to Christianity, finished his speech opposing the motion by saying, why did not Mr Massey go the whole-hog and rid the English language of all references to 'the Mass'; then he could be known as 'Mr Tidy'! The motion was defeated.

The Consumer's Christmas starts at the beginning of November, when the shops put up their decorations and start playing carols and Christmas music over the PA systems. Christmas shopping has begun. It ends on Christmas Eve as the *Sale* notices go up and the decorations come down. For most shoppers *Advent* is only a word associated with calendars with pieces of chocolate behind 24 apertures. The designers of these calendars reveal their ignorance of the meaning of the Christmas season by decorating the calendars with Disney comic characters or Father Christmas.

The tension

The Christian Christmas begins when Advent ends, namely on 24 December; it then continues until the feast of the Epiphany on 6 January. (In some traditions Christmastide concludes with Candlemas, the Presentation of the Lord, on 2 February.) There is a necessary and intended tension between the penitential aspect of Advent, being a season of preparation, and the joyous celebration of the Nativity.

There is a more obvious tension between the secular and the religious understanding and celebration of Christmas. This can be experienced in parishes and certainly in Church schools. If Advent is going to be observed properly then Christmas cannot be celebrated much before 25 December. This, of course, raises issues like when to put up decorations, when to give gifts and the singing of carols. In the school where I teach, we have had conflict and strong feelings expressed by pupils and some staff because the Head has insisted that Advent be kept properly. No Christmas decorations or carols are allowed in school until the last few days of term. The Head teacher's point is that if we surrender to the consumer's Christmas and celebrate as we shop, then the spiritual value of the *waiting* of Advent is lost.

Marking time

The word *Advent* comes from the Latin word *adventus* which means 'coming'. This refers, of course, to the coming of Christ, but, as we shall see, there is more than one coming. Advent suggests the passing of time and it is customary to use the burning of a candle, or a calendar, to mark off the days of this season of waiting.

Calendars exist to mark the passing of time. They hang in our kitchens and offices to remind us of coming events, a birthday, a dentist appointment or a weekend away. If it is an event we are not looking forward to, like the dentist appointment, we watch its gradual approach with secret dread! And it arrives all too soon. If it is a happy event, like a holiday, time seems to take longer in passing. But before we know it, the event is passed; and we are looking back at the calendar to remember when it was that we went to the dentist. We are creatures of time; it governs our lives completely.

Old photos of family and friends remind us, too uncomfortably, of the passing of time. We are sadly reminded of the inevitable shortness of life and therefore of the value of time: one of our most precious gifts. It's a fanciful thought, but if photographs of God were possible (I'm not talking here about Jesus, but about the Infinite Power and Source of all being to whom we give the name *God*) a photograph taken ten-thousand-years ago, or one-hundred-million-years ago, would look exactly the same as one taken today. God, of course, has no body and therefore, as a spirit (or rather as *the* Spirit) is not bound by time. God has no limits; He doesn't grow old. Minutes, hours, days, weeks, months, and even thousands of passing years, have no effect upon him. He is outside time and he doesn't need a calendar!

We start a new calendar year on 1 January with parties and fireworks to welcome in the New Year. It has meaning for us, but not for God. Every day is the same for him; every day is *now*.

We start a new Christian Year with the first Sunday of Advent, but it still has no effect upon God. It is still *now* for him. Even the Church's holy seasons do nothing to or for God. The Church's Year is not for his benefit but for ours; it is we who need to sign and mark the passing of time. The sacred seasons are there to help us draw closer in love and service to the Father, through the Son by the power of the Holy Spirit.

Time started when God decided to create; before that there was no time. The motion of God's creation, the sun, the planets and the earth with its moon, measures time. So creation and time are interwoven. The moment that God said, 'Let there be light', time began and has flowed on ever since. The twelve months of our calendar, from January to December, measure the motion of our solar system, which we experience as time.

Advent is the season most associated with the passing of time and creation; a period of patient waiting, of expectation and hope.

Love is God

On an inside page the *Daily Mail* of 20 December 1997 carried the banner heading 'The girl in a cage' and a three-quarter-page photograph of the four-year-old little girl sitting and crying in a wooden cage. The news report went on –

'The torment is etched on her face as she stares out from the tiny cage that has been her home for two years. Even if she were a dog, the treatment meted out to Lourdes Gomez would be considered barbaric. When she was two, Lourdes was locked in the bamboo prison by her parents simply for being a "nuisance".

'There she stayed – suspended above a pigsty – until a visitor to her parents spotted her shivering in the cold and alerted police in Mexico's central state of San Luis Potosi.'

The child has been taken into care and the parents are to stand trial. We are rightly outraged when we read or hear of such treatment meted out to children, for we know how children need love and care.

We would have known virtually nothing about our timeless God if it had not been for his coming among us as Jesus of Nazareth. You cannot get to know an un-approachable Spirit, the Power of Being and Consciousness, but you can get to know a human like yourself. A human person born into a family, like ourselves. Affected by the passing of time, like ourselves. Needing to love and be loved, like ourselves.

As we cannot talk about 'the year' without speaking about 'time', so we cannot think about 'the family' without considering 'love'. The child, who is the fruit of the love of a couple for one another, cannot grow to maturity without loving care; without receiving love and learning how to bestow it.

Surely the greatest revelation of the Good News from Jesus, God-among-us, was this, 'God is love' (1 John 4:16). You and I may *have* love in our hearts for our children, our parents, our friends; but while we *have* such a love, God *is* love. God does not possess love as an emotion or a virtue, like we do; he *is* love. I can say 'I am a man', but I cannot say 'I am love' because it is not my nature. Poor Lourdes Gomez may have had no experience of love and not know how to love, but she remains a human being; a neglected and impoverished human being. Of God alone can it be said that he *is* love.

Love must give

I have three teenage daughters and it has been a regular experience to have one or another of them agonising over the fickleness of the various specimens of manhood that they have brought to the house! 'But he said he loved me; now he can't even be bothered to phone!' *'You don't bring me flowers any more'*. so the words of the song go. A sure sign of the departure of love in human relationships is the absence of *giving*. An unwillingness to give not only gifts, but time and attention to another.

So one of the great characteristics of human love, recognised by us all, is the need to give. When a couple are in love they shower gifts on one another, are constantly on the phone (Oh, those phone bills!) and round one another's homes. God who *is* love is even more superlative in His gift-giving. 'God so loved the world that he gave us his one and only Son' (John 3:16). The celebration of that amazing gift-giving by love is what we prepare for during the four weeks of Advent.

God steps into time

At a moment in history there was a meeting between 'Time' and 'Love'. He who existed outside time stepped into human history. The result was a weak helpless baby.

Note that God could have come out of the desert as a fully-formed, mature and totally independent human person. Or he could have appeared as a king or great statesman. He could have been born into a royal court or as the child of a famous person of the time. But he had no interest in power, wealth or fame; they are human aberrations!

Love chose a poor and totally unknown loving couple to act as his human parents and role models. In the famous words of Christina Rossetti, 'Love came down at Christmas'. When by far the greatest and most incredible event in human history happened; when the Creator of the boundless universe with its billions of galaxies and countless stars and planets became a creature, that's how he came. God came among us as a weak and helpless baby dependent upon the loving care of a simple homeless couple.

It is almost too wonderful to take in; and that is what we are preparing, through Advent, to celebrate once again.

The Coming season

In the Church's season of 'the Coming', we find not one meeting of 'Love' and 'Time', prepared for and celebrated, but three. The liturgy of Advent speaks of the three 'Comings' of Jesus. This can be a little confusing, unless clearly spelt out and thought about; this is our task in the following chapters.

- The first Coming of 'Love' – as a baby – the first appearance among us; the Word made flesh and dwelling among us. Completely human but still totally divine. Jesus as a member of a human family.

- The second Coming of 'Love' – as the Word of God proclaimed – the appearance among us of the Christ, Jesus the preacher, revealing God's love to us.

14

- The third Coming of 'Love' – as the judge – the final Coming of Christ at the end of our time, and the world's time, as a loving and merciful judge.

In the four weeks of Advent these three 'Comings' of Christ are recalled by the liturgy of the Church. We will follow not the chronological order, as given above, but the spiritual order given to us by the Church's liturgy.

Summary

Advent is the 'Coming season' when, preparing for the Feast of the Incarnation, we recall Almighty God's incredible love. A love which prompted him to come among us as a human person. The Apostle John tells us that 'God *is* love'; so God was driven by his very nature to come to the aid of his creatures.

In our modern consumer society there are two conflicting 'Christmasses'; that of the shops and consumerism and that of the Christian faith. The Christian Christmas is preceded by the penitential season of Advent. Christmas begins on the evening of 24 December and continues until 6 January, the Feast of the Epiphany.

The Church's season of Advent prepares us not just for the coming of 'Love' as a tiny helpless baby, but also for Christ's coming as teacher, guide and judge.

Bible reading

Isaiah 9:2-7
(Alternatives: Jeremiah 33:14-16 or Micah 5:1-4)

Discussion points

1. *(After introductions around the group, the leader asks each participant in turn the following question. Discussion may follow after each has made a contribution.)*
   What *one* new idea or insight about Advent or Christmas did you get from reading the above material?

2. Do you agree or disagree that there are two Christmasses these days? Or has it always been like that? Does it matter? Should Christians fight it or 'go with it'?

3. Would most Christians be surprised to learn that Christmas was not celebrated for the first three hundred years of the Christian faith? What would it be like to return to those days? Would we be spiritually richer or poorer for a return to the early Church's total concentration upon Easter?

4. One Catholic bishop has directed his parish priests *not* to allow the singing of carols during Advent. What do you think? Should Christmas carols, which of course celebrate the birth of Jesus, be sung during the penitential season while we are preparing for the coming of Christ as a child or should thay be reserved for Christmas?

5 Advent is the season when we enter into the sense of longing and expectancy experienced by the Jewish people as they looked for the birth of the Messiah; how best can we do that? Now fasting is no longer required of us by the Church what might we do to make Advent special and penitential?

Prayer

O God, our loving Father,
> we thank you for giving us your Son
> to be the light of our world.

As we light our Advent candles
> and open the doors of our Advent calendars,
> help us gradually to open our minds and hearts
> to his coming.

Your love came as a baby,
> may we cherish our children and our families.

Your love came as a preacher
> proclaiming the Good News of salvation;
> may we cherish our Christian faith and share it.

Your love will come again as judge at the end of time;
> may we cherish and follow your law of love;
> may we always walk in the light of the same
> Christ our Lord.

Amen.

First week of Advent ⎯⎯⎯⎯⎯⎯

⎯⎯⎯⎯⎯⎯⎯⎯⎯ *Love comes as judge*

I had got back to Southend Central station from London, in the late afternoon, earlier than I had anticipated; all my transport connections had gone like clockwork and I only needed a bus home to complete a successful day. Opposite me, as I stood at the stop for my No. 2 bus, was the large car park, situated next to the Warrior Square Swimming Pool. More directly opposite, on the edge of the car park, was a very tall pole, on the top of which was a security camera. As I waited for my rather late bus, I watched the camera move slowly, sweeping the car park for any anti-social behaviour. It looked up Chichester Road and down towards the Bus Station. As it slowly turned to observe where I was standing I suddenly decided to wave to it! With a full-arm wave I gave the camera something to look at! It slowly swept past me; stopped; returned a little to check what it had seen, then moved from side to side three times; paused and continued on it's way. The camera had 'waved' back to me! I was a little embarrassed and looked round to see if anyone had been watching. Fortunately no one had and at that point my No. 2 arrived.

Three days later I learnt from a friend that the security camera was operated from the Civic Centre, about a mile away, by disabled people. As I reflected on this unexpected occurrence it seemed to me rather a good parallel to our relationship with God. Like the camera operator, God is unseen and we so often experience him as 'distant'. A wave is a cheery greeting, a sign. The unseen camera operator had 'waved' back, as best he or she could, using a sign to acknowledge my greeting. My cheerful 'spirit' had communicated by moving my arm to and fro; the personality or 'spirit' of the operator had used a corresponding sign to respond. Presumably a miserable operator would have dismissed my wave as 'stupid antics'.

Then there was the thought of the ancient symbol for God, as the all-seeing eye; a large, wide-open eye that represented the all-seeing, all-knowing God. The story is told of a child who, when confronted with this symbol of God, told a priest that it was 'spooky' and 'scary', and began to cry. The priest consoled her, telling her not to cry but to think of her mother. 'Think of your mum', he said, 'when you were very little didn't she keep an eye on you, all the time, to check that you were safe? That was the loving eye of your mum. God is your caring Father and he has his loving eye on you all the time; he loves you so much that he can't take his eyes off you!' The child understood and smiled; a simple lesson that not every adult has understood.

God is unknowable, except through what he chooses to reveal about himself. He has communicated and continues to communicate, people with faith believe, through the use of signs. For example, on occasion he has used fire and wind. Immediately there comes to mind the experience of Elijah on the mountainside: 'Go out and stand on the mountainside in the presence of the Lord, for the Lord is about to pass by' (1 Kings 19:11-13). Then a great and powerful wind tore the mountains apart and shattered the rocks; but the Lord was not in the wind. After the wind there was an earthquake, but the Lord was not in the earthquake. After the earthquake came a fire, but the Lord was not in the fire. And after the fire came a gentle whisper . . . God was not in the fearful and obvious signs of power, the powerful wind and the earthquake, but in the gentle whisper!

One of the biggest and most common mistakes that we make is to look for God in the wrong places. We think, well, he's all powerful, almighty and all-knowing so he must be incredibly splendid. A cathedral, at least, is the right place to look. But no, he is closer than that! It is nicely put in this piece by Brenda Rogers.

I was dusting the bedroom when I discovered God,
I've often looked for him, or it, before,
upstairs, downstairs, in my lady's chamber,
but never there where I found it –
    Last place you'd think to look!
Don't think I'm going to tell you right away
where I found it!
After all, it took me forty years,
so why should I make it easy for you?
You can damn well wait for a couple more lines at least.
Well now, where was I?
Oh, yes, in the bedroom
discovering God.
Well, where do you think it was then?
I'll bet you'll never guess.
It was here in me all the time!
(Like Maeterlinck's Blue Bird
poignantly sitting at home –
That was a heartbreaker film for me to see
when I was an evacuee)

Funny really
Doesn't seem to equate with housework
    me walking round with the Godhead inside me.
I went in Woolworth's later,
met several friends
but it didn't seem to show.

Just as well, really:
After all, they never show theirs to me.
Brenda Rogers

We have got to get our ideas straight about where God can be found (not that he's limited, of course, to any one place) because this is the God who is our judge, as referred to in the readings of the First Sunday of Advent. If we picture God as Judge, sitting in awesome splendour up in the clouds, waiting to condemn us to some fearful fate, we may have a few spiritual difficulties.

Many popular performers, like Dionne Warwick, Cliff Richard and others have recorded the popular song *From A Distance*. It is often used in secondary school assemblies, because the words *God is watching us from a distance* seem to speak of God's loving care. This is not however a truly Christian approach. God is not distant from us; on the contrary, he is closer to us than we are to ourselves. Before the Incarnation, when *'the Word was made flesh and dwelt among us'* (John 1:14), that could have been believed; but since that most amazing of events in human history, God is here among us. The risen Christ said, 'I shall be with you always, even to the end of time' (Matthew 28:20). St Paul left us those memorable words, 'I live, now not I, Christ lives in me' (Galatians 2:20).

The Gospel of St John and his letters are full of wonderful references to God's love and presence within us. Here are just three:

- 'If anyone loves me, he will obey my teaching. My Father will love him, and we will come to him and make our home with him' (John 14:23).

- 'No one has ever seen God; but if we love one another, God lives in us and his love is made complete in us' (1 John 4:12).

- 'God is love. Whoever lives in love lives in God, and God in him' (1 John 4:16).

The morning after I wrote the above paragraph, I received a phone call at 4.30am. The voice on the phone informed me that she was the duty matron of Magnolia Nursing Home, at Barling, and that 82-year-old Mrs Rene Montague had died half an hour earlier. I had taken her Holy Communion not many hours before, late on the Sunday morning, and she had been very poorly, agitated and confused; a state she had been in for nearly two weeks. Rene had been continually depressed ever since her husband died, two years before, and regularly stated that she wanted to join him. When I visited her, in those last few days, she had said more than once, 'Why doesn't he (Christ) come for me?' As I put the phone down that morning, I thought, 'and now he has'. Christ had often come to her in Holy Communion, but Rene had in mind his final coming.

I could not return to bed after that news and sat quietly over a cup of tea in the kitchen. It occurred to me that even as I was receiving the news of her death, Rene was in the presence of the Christ whom she had devoutly loved and served for many years. Her judgement had already taken place. And so it will be with us all! According to traditional Christian belief there will be first a personal meeting with Christ, our judge; then, one day at the end of time, the general judgement.

In the early 1960s a revolution took place in Christian prayer in Britain, and throughout Europe. It was sparked off by the book *Prayers of Life* by a French priest from Le Havre, Michel Quoist. It was published in twenty five languages and sold seven million copies. It was so popular because it liberated many Christians, of various denominations, from rigid, formalised forms of prayer. It was the first of a flood of books that appeared, showing how we can all pray from, and about, the very ordinary things of life, in our own words. Michel Quoist died on 18 December 1997 at the age of 76. In his last book, *Construire l'Homme,* he chose to reprint a prayer written some 40 years ago which expressed his confidence that eventually everything does make sense and is a coherent whole. It is a matter of perspective. Ultimately all of creation is progressing towards its creator, who sanctifies all he has made.

Death will bring understanding, Michel Quoist says. Everything, simply everything, is sacred and precious to God and all leads inevitably to the Godhead, the Holy Trinity. Death will put everything into its proper perspective.

Do we have to wait for that uncertain hour; for that unwelcome moment in our personal history? Can we not benefit now?

Very many years ago, when I was 11-years-old, I took the eleven plus selective exam, as it was in those days. Would I pass and go to the Dover Grammar School for boys, or would I fail and go to the local county secondary school? I had, even at that tender age, the great desire to be a priest and I was informed that it was necessary to go to the grammar school, if I was to go on to the priesthood. So it appeared obvious to me, as I firmly believed that I had a vocation to the priesthood, that God intended me to pass the exam and go to the Dover Grammar. I prayed hard that I would pass and really believed that God would hear my prayer. Imagine my surprise when I learnt that I had failed! I had to go instead to Castlemount County Secondary and I hated it. Two years later, I was accepted for the Junior Seminary of St Joseph's, at Mark Cross in Kent.

As the years passed, I found myself teaching at a secondary school, dealing with youngsters who had had their self-confidence destroyed, nursing a sense of failure, because they had failed the eleven plus exam (retained in our corner of Essex until very recently). I discovered that I was ideally placed to reassure them, to reveal the injustice of such a selective process and help them to re-build their confidence and self-esteem. In addition, I now believe that, if I had gone to the Dover Grammar school, I would never have gone to the Seminary and received an education in theology and spirituality. Two good reasons why, in retrospect, God did not answer my prayers. He knew better; he knew what lay ahead and what benefits could come from my failure.

So it is with much of our lives; when we look back we can see meaning and purpose when, at the time, there appears to be none. Here lies the point and value of Michel Quoist's insight. If we are going to be prepared, at death, for Christ when he comes for us, we must be courageously realistic, and learn to put everything into its proper perspective.

On a recent BBC Radio 4 programme, an elderly gentleman was being interviewed about his pension and life insurance policy. In answer to a question about the terms of his life policy he replied, 'If anything happens to me the money will go to my daughter'. What's this about *if*, when he means, *'when* I die the money will . . .'? The first step in preparation for the meeting with our judge, when he comes, is to accept, fully and completely, that my death is going to happen and that the meeting is really going to take place.

Jesus, in our Gospel reading (Matthew 24:42), tells us to 'stay awake!' He instructs us to be alert and prepared, 'because you do not know when the master of the house (Christ himself) is coming'. We all know relatives, friends and acquaintances, of all ages and states of life, who have died suddenly and unexpectedly. This is what shook the nation over the death of Diana, Princess of Wales. So being prepared is not something to be left to some indefinite time in the future.

We do not have to be morbid and frightened by these thoughts, if we take seriously and work at the second step in our preparation. Once we have accepted that 'the time *will* come', and we need to be prepared, that will give a meaning and purpose to our lives. Then we have to be alert and attentive ('stay awake') to Christ's presence within. In her poem, Brenda Rogers shares with us her wonder at finding God's presence within her. (*It might be a good idea to re-read it.*) That is an essential discovery that we all need to make. If we get to know and develop our relationship with Christ dwelling within us now, then we will have nothing to fear when he comes as judge.

There is that rather unfunny joke about the man who was seen occasionally at the back of the church on a Sunday. When asked by an usher why he would not accept a hymn book and take a fuller part in the service, the man replied, 'I just look in occasionally so that when I get to the pearly gates God will recognise me and not ask who I am'!

If Christ becomes the intimate friend within, when he comes for us at the end, in the role of judge, it will not be a fearsome experience, but the face to face meeting of old and familiar friends.

Summary

God can seem to be distant and remote from us; it is true that, as creator, he does transcend all that exists in the universe. However it is equally true that God is also within his creation and within us. We need to seek his presence, not away in the skies but within our very selves. God knows all, sees all; but his all-seeing eye is the loving eye of the caring parent.

At death Christ comes for us and we meet him as our judge. This will be, for you and me, our first personal face-to-face encounter with Christ, his *first* coming to us. We need not fear this judgement for, if we now wish it, it can be the meeting of old friends. Christ lives now, by faith, in our hearts; we only need to become attentive to this presence and build our lives upon it.

Bible reading

Mark 13:33-37
(Alternatives: Matthew 24:37-44 or Luke 21:25-28; 34-36)

Discussion points

1. Have you ever realised that the Gospel readings for Advent point not just to the coming of Jesus as a baby at Christmas, but lead us to think about the three 'Comings' of Christ?

2. How do you picture, or imagine, God? A distant, ancient, father-figure sitting on a throne up in the clouds? Or a celestial policeman who keeps a watchful eye on us to see that we are keeping all the rules? (*The group will benefit from sharing insights at this point.*)

3. *Someone reads aloud Brenda Rogers' poem.* What do you think of the poem? Is it helpful? Does it raise questions or answer some inner thoughts we have had? Which New Testament text does it illustrate practically?

4. Would any member of the group like to share an experience or insight which has come later in life to clarify and bring a deeper understanding of, and meaning to, some past 'failure' or event?

5. Is it true that people are inclined to believe that they are invincible, death will not touch them, or are they too frightened to accept that it will happen to them? What should be the Christian approach to death?

6. Is it helpful to realise that the Christ who is with me, at this very moment, is the same person who will review my life with me, at the end? In what ways can we deepen our knowledge and our love of the Christ who dwells within?

Prayer

Lord God
  We adore you
    because you have come to us in the past.
  You have spoken to us
    in the Law of Israel.
  You have challenged us
    in the words of the Prophets.
  You have shown us in Jesus
    what you are really like.

Lord God
  We adore you
    because you still come to us now.
  You come to us through other people
    and their love and concern for us.
  You come to us through men and women
    who need our help.
  You come to us as we worship you
    with your people.

Lord God
  We adore you
    because you will come to us at the end.
  You will be with us
    at the hour of death.
  You will still reign supreme
    when all human institutions fail.
  You will still be God
    when our history has run its course.

We welcome you,
 the God who comes.
Come to us now
 in the power of Jesus Christ our Lord.
Amen.

Second week of Advent ──────────

────────── *Love comes as Messiah and teacher*

'Prepare the way'

To appreciate the following story you have to know that I act in a voluntary capacity, when I am not at my full-time employment or pursuing the role of husband and father, as Pastoral Lay Assistant in my parish. The parish divides naturally into three parts, each with its own church; so there are three lay assistants supporting the work of the one parish priest. We each act as leader of our local area, visit the sick, take the occasional Holy Communion or prayer service in the area church and form part of the Parish Pastoral Team.

Close to my home, until a year ago, lived a middle-aged couple, whose four young adult children had all flown the nest. Hilda was a devout Catholic and her husband, Len, was a staunch atheist, although he had never stood in the way of Hilda practising her faith or bringing up the children as Catholics. Len had retired from the Air Force and then worked for some years at Southend Airport. From early in their marriage he had been a popular figure in the bar, any bar, and a well-known womaniser. He would disappear for the occasional night and, without explanation, for the odd weekend! After his retirement from the RAF his drinking and unfaithfulness did not improve. Hilda's friends repeatedly advised her to leave him, but she would always declare that she would stick by her marriage vows; she believed that, in his own way, Len still loved her and would one day need her.

In his early fifties Len was forced to give up work, as his life style had damaged his health; after a while he was also discovered to have cancer. Unable now to go out he would sit slumped all day despondently in front of the TV screen, still smoking and drinking. Life with him was not easy, but Hilda bore it cheerfully.

I had not called at their house for some time, when a mutual friend rang me to let me know that Len was very poorly and had been admitted to hospital. It was a Thursday evening and I went round to see Hilda, who had just returned from the hospital. She confirmed that Len was very ill; I promised to visit him on Saturday morning. However, early on Saturday morning, she rang me from the hospital to tell me that Len had just died peacefully. She said it would mean a lot to her and the family if I would come up to the hospital and say a prayer over Len. I agreed to do this, on condition that the parish priest gave his approval. Five minutes later, with his approval, I was on my way.

When I stepped into the hospital room, I found the family gathered around Len's body; Hilda was clearly pleased to see me. I sat by the body and read a few appropriate prayers; I concluded with the family saying the Lord's Prayer together. When I stepped back from the body, I said a word or two to Hilda and gave her a hug. She then asked, 'Did I do the right thing?'

'What was that?' I asked.

'Well, late last evening I was sitting by Len, who had been unconscious or sleeping much of the day. He opened his eyes and said, 'I'm dying, aren't I?' I replied, 'Yes, dear'.

'Would you say some prayers with me?' he whispered. Hilda told me the prayers that she had said, then added, 'He drifted into unconsciousness after a few minutes and he never woke up again; and I did it!' Intrigued I asked, 'What did you do?' Hilda explained, 'I got a bowl and a glass of water and I baptised him! Did I do right?'

'Yes' I said, with no hesitation. 'Len showed that he had faith by asking you to pray with him. And you have enough faith for the both of you.' That helped Hilda immensely in her grief.

There can be no doubt that the faith, love and devotion of Hilda finally brought her husband to God and saved him.

This week we encounter the wild figure of John the Baptiser 'proclaiming a baptism of repentance'. He was not out to claim people for God, for they were already believing Jews, but to re-claim them. Before the Messiah (the Christ) could come among them they had to be prepared; they had to be receptive.

Len, in our story, was more receptive to accepting that he needed a relationship with God than he knew. Gradually, imperceptibly, over the years, Hilda's loving service, her faith and her faithfulness must have 'spoken' to him; softening him at his deepest level. I had always been rather uneasy with Len's arrogant, know-it-all, attitude to life; he was inclined to be a little condescending to active church members like myself.

This was the very challenge that John, son of Zechariah, faced. The Jews of his time, who came in curiosity from Jerusalem, fifteen miles away, to hear him preach, were arrogant about their religious adherence. They acted in a very superior fashion, with their 'We are the Chosen People of God' routine. They were implying that all others, especially the Romans and the Samaritans, were nothing but scum! John tells them roundly and forcibly, 'Don't presume to tell yourselves, "we have Abraham for our father", because I tell you, God can raise children for Abraham from these stones'.

John is looking for a change of heart; he demands some sign of humility, as an indication that they are really repentant and receptive. If you are really sorry and genuinely want to prepare for the coming of the Messiah, come down here in the river, he says to them, and I will humble you, by plunging you under the water.

The second 'Coming' of Advent, the Coming of Love as Messiah and teacher, demands a humble openness. No arrogance will accept the Christ of love. (Many years later, John the Gospel-writer, sadly records, 'He came to his own people, and his own people did not accept him' – John 1:11). At his birth the Word of God arrives among us as a totally helpless baby; born in someone else's stable. At his death he is the victim of rejection and an unjust death penalty; buried in someone else's tomb.

When the Messiah appears on the banks of the Jordan he is one of the crowd, asking for and receiving baptism, like everyone else. There is not an ounce of arrogance and pride in Jesus of Nazareth. Those who desire to be his friends must have, or at least be aware that they must strive for, a sense of humility. 'What I have done for you', Jesus said during the Last Supper, after washing his friends' feet, 'you must do for one another.'

Near Maldon, in Essex, there is the Orthodox monastery of St John the Baptist. For eleven years I have made an annual visit there, in July, with my students who are in Year 12 and studying for their 'A' level Religious Studies exam. Every year we are welcomed and shown round by Sister Magdalene, a highly educated and articulate member of the mixed community. We are only at the monastery for two-and-a-half hours, but for me it is like having a whole day's retreat. The atmosphere is so peaceful and prayerful. The monastery, which was originally an old Anglican vicarage with extensive grounds, was founded in 1959 by a very holy Orthodox monk, the Archimandrite Sophrony. He died, well into his nineties, only a few years ago. In my last visit to the monastery, before his death, when he was very poorly, Sister Magdalene spoke of his condition. She told us that the Abbot thought that he ought to tell Father Sophrony that he was dying. The old monk replied, 'You must be mistaken, Father Abbot, because I am not humble enough yet to die'.

I have read several of Father Sophrony's books, and he is, at present, my favourite spiritual writer. His own spiritual guide and mentor, Father Silouan, who was a monk of Mount Athos in Greece, died in 1938. He was declared a saint just a few years ago; shortly before Father Sophrony's death. The patron saint of their monastery is well chosen for throughout Father Sophrony's writings runs the theme of repentance and humility. He writes in *We Shall See Him As He Is.*

> 'When I measure myself against the commandments of Christ – to love God with all one's being and one's neighbour as oneself – I do not possess the means to judge how far I am from my purpose. And it seems then that I still have not acquired repentance, though its flame has touched me and made itself known.'

The purpose of Advent is that the flame of repentance may touch us and we may respond. The colour of 'the flame', if we can speak like that, is purple, the Advent liturgical colour for repentance and humility. When the season was first introduced into the life of the Church, some time in the fifth century, it was six weeks in length and there was fasting on Mondays, Wednesdays and Fridays. Like Lent, which is some two hundred years older, and on which Advent is modelled, the entire purpose of Advent was to fast in preparation for the coming Feast of the Incarnation.

We can catch something of the early understanding of Advent from these, rather quaint, words of Hugh of St Victor, a German monk of the Middle Ages, who lived 850 years ago.

> 'Brothers and sisters, it is now the season of the Lord's coming, and we must use the time to prepare ourselves by some spiritual devotion. We must strive to enter the house of our hearts, open the windows, and notice what is seemly and what is unseemly in that house. We must brush away the cobwebs, sweep the floors, clear out the dust and dirt, strew the clean floors with freshly gathered rushes, fragrant herbs and sweet-smelling flowers.'

Father Sophrony expressed the belief, even after many years of prayer and self-denial, 'I still have not acquired repentance'. It seems a little surprising to ordinary Christians like us, that holy people can write such things. They truly believe themselves to be 'the worst of sinners'. Surely, we think, they are close to God and have put that part of their lives well behind them.

This apparent contradiction was once explained to me like this. If you are walking in a street, where there is just the occasional street light, there are areas of light, under the lamp, and areas of darkness between the lamps. Between the two it is very shadowy. Every detail of a person can only be seen when he or she is standing close to a light, but only the general outline of a person in the unlit area. The person in the dark area is walking towards the light and can see sufficiently, although not yet in the full light. In the same way the saint is closer to Christ the Light of the World than we are and can see the real state of themselves. Whereas we, who are still journeying in the dark towards the light, are happy enough with ourselves, because we cannot see the true state of our spiritual lives.

'God is light; in him there is no darkness at all. If we claim to have fellowship with him yet walk in the darkness, we lie and do not live by the truth. But if we walk in the light, as he is in the light, we have fellowship with one another, and the blood of Jesus, his Son, purifies us from all sin' (1 John 1:5-7).

Humility is just that, seeing ourselves as Christ sees us; not as we imagine ourselves to be. As we grow closer to Christ in love, we will gradually see and accept that not all is well in our relationship with God and our neighbour.

How are we really, now, today, meeting the challenge 'to love God with all our being and our neighbour as ourself'?

It is so easy to deceive ourselves; that is why, when it is

possible, anyone who is serious about developing a spiritual life finds a spiritual counsellor or director to guide them. Most of us cannot do that easily, but we can take full advantage of the liturgical year and make the most of Advent and Lent. These are times when the opportunity is provided, by the Church, to review our lives, to admit courageously that we sin, in lots of small ways, every day. The impatient word, the half-truth, the boastful comment dropped into conversation, the mingy response to a charitable appeal, the spreading of gossip, the lack of generosity in giving time to prayer. The list is almost endless, once we start being brutally honest with ourselves.

> 'If we claim to be without sin, we deceive ourselves and the truth is not in us. If we confess our sins, he is faithful and just and will forgive us our sins and purify us from all unrighteousness. If we claim we have not sinned, we make him out to be a liar and his word has no place in our lives' (1 John 1:8-10).

It was precisely because John the Baptist wanted the words of Christ, when he came as a teacher, to find a place in the hearts and minds of the Jewish people that he preached so energetically and exhorted them to set aside their arrogant attitude and have a *change of heart*; the meaning of the word *metanoia* (repent) used by John.

The Jewish people did not recognise the role of John, son of Zechariah, any more than they recognised and understood the role of Jesus, the Son of God. If they had realised that John, because he prepared the way for the Messiah and his teaching, was, in the words of Jesus, the greatest human ever born (see Matthew 11:11) they would never have allowed King Herod to execute him. If the Jewish religious authorities had understood the mission of John and had been more faithful to the Scriptures, then they would not have dared to have Jesus the Messiah executed. On both occasions they were guilty of spiritual blindness. In Advent, and at all times, we must use every opportunity to try to see ourselves as we really are; as God sees us. Then the words of the Messiah will take root in our hearts.

Let us conclude this chapter with a favourite story of mine that gave me much to think about, as I helped to bring up four children. A little boy of five was left alone with his father at bedtime. It had never happened before. After some manoeuvring and a lot of fun, the father finally got the little fellow into his night clothes, and was about to lift him into bed when the child said, 'But daddy, I have to say my prayers'. He knelt down beside his bed, joined his hands, raised his eyes to heaven and prayed: 'Now I lay me down to sleep, I pray the Lord my soul to keep; if I should die before I wake, I pray the Lord my soul to take.' That was his usual prayer, but tonight he looked up at his dad, then raised his eyes to heaven again and prayed, 'Dear God, make me a great big, good man, like my daddy, Amen.' In a moment he was in bed, and in five minutes asleep. And then the father knelt by his son's bedside and prayed, 'Dear Lord, make me a great big, good man like my boy thinks I am.' P. Fontaine

Summary

John the Baptist appealed to the Jews of his time to put aside their arrogance and humbly admit that they sinned; a sign of that repentance was entering the Jordan for the ritual sign of baptism. Christ the preacher, who brought the words of God, could not come and deliver his message, unless people were humbly receptive.

It is no different today. If Christ's Good News is going to be accepted and acted upon there has to be faith, honesty and openness. The biggest problem that even practising Christians have is to be totally honest and open. Every one of us is capable of self-deception; the only remedy is to be regularly reviewing our lives and daily asking God's forgiveness.

Bible reading

Matthew 3:1-12 or Mark 1:1-8

Discussion points

1. Do you think that Hilda acted correctly by baptising her husband? Did you realise that any Christian, in an emergency, can conduct a baptism?

2. John the Baptiser uses the word *metanoia* (repent). What was he looking for from those who came to hear him preach? Why?

3. The Jewish people of the time, like many religious people, considered themselves better than others, because they kept exactly the many religious laws. What did Jesus have to say about such an approach? Are we ever in danger of spiritual arrogance?

4. What indications are there to suggest that Jesus of Nazareth was very humble? Does this conflict with his role?

5. Can you suggest reasons why people who are close to God constantly feel the need to repent daily of their sins?

6. *(Someone read out the words of Hugh of St Victor.)* Allowing for the different cultural setting of these words, do you think they give us some useful advice on the importance of Advent?

7. Can Christ come and be welcomed by those who are self-sufficient, proud and unwilling to admit that they are wrong?

8. How best can we have a 'change of heart' in Advent? Do we have to find new ways or are there already opportunities which we are not using fully or properly?

Prayer

Let me love you, Christ my Lord,
   in your first Coming,
   when you were made man
   for love of mankind,
   and for love of me.

Let me love you, Christ my Lord,
   in your second Coming,
   when, with unimaginable love,
   you stand at the door and knock,
   and would enter into our hearts,
   and into mine.

Plant in my soul, Christ my Lord,
   the likeness of your love,
   that, when death calls,
   it may be ready
   and burning
   to come to you.
Amen.

Third week of Advent

Love comes as teacher and model

One of my most cherished memories is of my grandfather, whom I dearly loved, working in his smithy. He was a wheelwright, a traditional craftsman, who was as skilled with the plane as with the hammer and anvil. Between the ages of seven and nine I would slip into his smithy whenever I could, to watch him at work, sparks flying as he hammered out a red-hot iron. Or he would be in the workshop delicately shaping a spoke with a spokeshave. I loved being with him; he would say little as he concentrated on his work, just getting me to give him a hand by pumping the long arm of the bellows up and down, which made the smithy fire glow when he needed it. Sometimes he would reward me with a thruppenny piece.

It is only in recent years that I have realised how skilful he really was, especially as I believe that the traditional method of making a wooden wheel with an iron rim has been all but lost. Now that I am at the age my grandfather was when I watched him, I wish I had been his apprentice and learned the ancient art. How satisfying it must have been, to take chunks of wood and lengths of iron and from them, with the skill handed on from father to son, the strength of your arm, the judgement of your eye, and a few simple tools, create a carriage wheel. Strong, perfectly balanced with shaped and decorated spokes.

I have some of my grandfather's tools; they are simple and ancient in form. The mallet, the hammer, the crossaw, the spokeshave, for example, have not changed for two thousand years. Jesus the craftsman would certainly recognise them and would have possessed the skill to use them. Did he know how to make a wooden wheel with an iron rim?

No one can come to a place without first leaving somewhere

else. Jesus could not have appeared in the crowds on the banks of the Jordan, listening to John and asking for baptism, if he had not first left his old life behind. One day he hung up his tools, looked round the simple workshop, and probably said to his mother, 'Sell the tools, they will bring you a little cash to keep you going'. He closed the rough door and left to become an itinerant preacher. (I wonder who had Jesus' tools and what eventually became of them!)

Although we have no record of Jesus writing anything (except 'on the ground with his finger' when the woman who had been caught committing adultery was brought to him, John 8:1-11) he was literate. Nazareth was a thoroughly Jewish settlement with approximately two-thousand inhabitants, which would have been sufficient to have and maintain at least one synagogue and rabbi; and that meant a school. The local boys, up to the age of 12 or 13, would have learned how to read the Hebrew Torah (the first five books of the Bible) and discuss it. According to St Luke, Jesus was particularly skilled at this by the time he left school (Luke 2:46). Jesus would have known three languages (more than I do!): Hebrew, for use in the synagogue worship; Aramaic, spoken at home and in village life; Greek, for the trips to the market place, where the passing traders would only have used the language common in the Empire at that time.

So when Jesus left home to walk to the place on the banks of the Jordan, some sixty-five miles away, where his cousin John was preaching, he was well equipped to start his own preaching mission. Humanly he had a thorough knowledge and experience of the problems of daily life (taxation running at forty-per-cent), sufficient literacy, a good grounding in the Scriptures and a deep prayer life. The Spirit of God prompts and leads him to believe that now is the time; God wants him to come among his people as the Messiah, *the* teacher, who will reveal God's love for the world; as *the* model of how to live in the love of God and neighbour. This is the *Coming* of Jesus that prompts you to read these words and make the most of the season of Advent. This is the *Coming* which touches our daily lives, as we struggle to live by his teaching, which we have freely accepted.

In the religious press recently there was the following story:

The first soldier saint of World War II may soon be canonised. In Italy squares, schools and streets are named after him; yet he is little known outside his native land.

Born in Naples, Salvo D'Aquisto at 18 joined the Carabinieri, the oldest regiment in the Italian Army. He enjoyed military life and, on the outbreak of war, he served for eighteen months in North Africa, on active service. Tall, athletic and handsome, 'a true son of Southern Italy', Salvo had a girlfriend, Maria, and was devout in the practice of his Catholic faith.

Italy changed sides in the war and Salvo, promoted to an NCO, was posted to a little village north of Rome. On Thursday, 23 September he went to confession, morning Mass and received Holy Communion. His commanding officer was absent so Salvo was the senior officer in the village, when a detachment of the German SS arrived. Salvo went out to greet them politely, but was struck and arrested.

The previous day the SS had occupied a medieval tower at nearby Palidoro; there had been an explosion that was later discovered to have been an accident. The SS, however, suspected sabotage. The SS commander rounded up 22 men of the village and threatened to kill them as a reprisal unless Salvo told him who was responsible for the explosion, which had killed one German soldier and wounded two others.

The prisoners were forced to dig a ditch, which was to

be their grave. Salvo kept calm and tried to reason with the SS commander. At 5pm he had persuaded him to release the 22 men; only one, a 17-year-old, to whom Salvo had been talking while they dug the ditch, stayed to see what happened. Salvo convinced the SS officer that if anyone was responsible, it must be his responsibility as officer in charge. Salvo was shot and buried in the ditch. He had said, earlier in the day, to the young man, 'You live once, you die once'.

A man of generosity, bravery and love. It is not likely that Salvo said to himself, 'I am inspired by the example of Jesus, who gave his life for others'; but it was the model of Jesus that he had been brought up to admire, and, in his final hours, imitate. Salvo's simple tomb is in the beautiful Santa Chiara church, in Naples. The words of Jesus come to mind, 'No greater love can a man have than to lay down his life'.

Love gives, love shares. God so loved the world that he shared himself with us in the person of his Son. Jesus came as a preacher to reveal God's love for us; however, we so easily think of the message, the content of what he had to say, and miss an important dimension. Jesus lived what he preached. Salvo did not rely on his words to the SS officer, he went one step further and offered himself.

An old friend of mine, Father John Medcalf, has recently returned from Latin America, where he worked for over twenty-five years in the shanty towns. I invited him to visit the school where I teach, to talk of his experiences to the senior students. Towards the end of a long session with the 'A' level students, a question from one of them revealed a total misunderstanding. Although Father John had spoken of the terrible living conditions in the vast shanty towns outside the big cities, the students had assumed that, being a priest, he had lived in the comfort of the city and driven out each day to work among the poor.

Father John gently corrected this mistake; the priests who volunteer to work among the poor of the favelas share their living conditions.

When Jesus started his preaching mission, he did not return to the comfort of his own home, and Mary's cooking, each evening; he left home never to return. He lived among the poor and destitute; he shared their life. When Jesus proclaimed the Good News, he lived it.

Jesus *is* the Good News. To hear Jesus was to hear God's word; to see Jesus in action was to see God in action. He did not just tell us to 'love God with our whole heart and our neighbour as ourselves'; he lived it. Jesus is God's gift to us.

'For God so loved the world that he gave his one and only Son, that whoever believes in him shall not perish but have eternal life' (John 3:16).

A wonderful example of transformation and total commitment for our Advent meditation and discussions, is the story of the famous Archbishop Oscar Romero.

The 'Monsignor', as his people liked to call him, was chosen and approved as the archbishop of San Salvador, and the leader of the Catholic Church in El Salvador, because he was a quiet academic, who was unlikely to question the policies of that country's National Security government. However, those policies were oppressive and corrupt. After his friend, Father Rutilio Grande, and several other priests, had been murdered by off-duty policemen, because they spoke up for the poor, Archbishop Romero changed. He became an outspoken champion of the poor and oppressed. He received many death threats from government agents (a government that was avowedly Christian!) and was eventually shot dead, on 24 March 1980, as he said Mass in the hospital chapel.

Like so many prophets before him, including John the Baptist and Jesus himself, he preached love and repentance and, as a result, met a violent death. He said, on one occasion,

> 'We have never preached violence, except the violence of love, which left Christ nailed to a cross, the violence that we must each do to ourselves is to overcome our selfishness.'

Of Advent Oscar Romero said:

> 'Advent should admonish us to discover
> in each brother and sister that we greet,
> in each friend whose hand we shake,
> in each beggar who asks for bread,
> in each worker who wants to use the right to join a union,
> in each peasant who looks for work in the coffee groves,
> the face of Christ.
>
> Then it would not be possible to rob them,
> to cheat them,
> to deny them their rights.
>
> They are Christ,
> and whatever is done to them
> Christ will take as done to him.
> That is what Advent is:
> Christ living among us.'

When Christ came as our teacher, he came for ever. He has never left us. He is with us when we read the New Testament, when we gather as 'two or three' in his name, when we share the Eucharist and, as Oscar Romero reminds us, in those around us; especially those who are, in any way, in need.

Summary

To take up his mission as teacher, and appear among the people as the Messiah, Jesus had to leave his old life behind. Literate and well-prepared, with a thorough knowledge of the Scriptures and a first-hand experience of a working life among impoverished people, Jesus came as God's voice. His message was not just an uplifting moral code, but he spoke with the authority of God. It was even more than that; the totality of the Good News was Christ himself; what he said, what he did and who he was.

His coming was at one moment in time; but he has never left us. He continues to speak to us, through the words of Scripture, through the Church, through the inspiration that comes from the Holy Spirit, through the love and service that we can give to others. He continues to inspire us, too, by the model of his life and his loving.

Bible reading

Matthew 11:2-11
(Alternatives: John 1:6-8; 19-28 or Luke 3:10-18)

Discussion points

1. Had you ever thought of how difficult it must have been for Jesus to 'hang up his tools' and say good-bye to his old life at Nazareth?

2. To leave a place and start a new life is usually not easy; have you ever had that experience? Could you share it with us?

3. A theologian has written, 'Jesus, the carpenter, did not, and could not, make perfect tables, but he could make them perfectly'; what belief is the writer conveying?

4. When Jesus came to the crowds, however, as teacher, he spoke with the authority of God. What responsibility does that lay upon the listeners? How can we receive that same teaching today?

5. Christ came to reveal God's love to us; in what ways did he do this? Do you think that, perhaps, we have given insufficient thought to Christ as our model?

6. Together let us take a look at the words of Oscar Romero and adapt and alter them to fit our own lives and experience.

Prayer

Grow, Jesus –
   grow in me –
In my mind, my heart,
   my imagination, my senses.
Grow by your purity,
   your zeal, your love.
Grow in me, Lord,
   with your grace, your light,
   your peace.
Grow in spite of my resistance,
   my pride.
Grow into the fullness of the
   Perfect one,
   as you grew at Nazareth –
   before God and all people –
For your Father's glory.
Amen.

Mother Magdalen Taylor

Fourth week of Advent

Love comes as helpless child

Our third child had an eventful arrival in the world. I was saved, by only a few minutes, from having to be the midwife! It happened in this fashion. Our eldest child was five at the time, and the second daughter was three; both had been late in arriving in the world. Liz, my wife, was a week away from the date given to her by the doctor for the arrival of number three. She had repeatedly (as wives do) asked me to get the cot down from the loft. I had excused myself from action by pointing out that there was plenty of time, as she was always late giving birth and it was planned that she would go into hospital for the delivery and return home twenty-four hours after baby's arrival.

On this particular Thursday evening my wife went to bed early and I sat up to watch a TV programme. When I went up to the bedroom at 11pm she was evidently in pain; but it passed quickly and she dismissed it as the 'baby having a practice session'. Ten minutes later it happened again; and Liz dismissed it with the comment that it was not painful enough to be more than a practice twinge. This was repeated again and again, with the length of time between gradually shortening. I insisted that I should ring Mrs King, the midwife, who was to accompany Liz into Rochford hospital for the delivery. My wife was adamant; 'I should know' she said, 'I've done this twice before and it is definitely not the real thing'. When it was close to 1am and the interval between contractions had got to three minutes, I ignored my wife and rang Mrs King. I told her the situation and said that she would be round immediately.

Fortunately she only lived about five hundred yards away and was at our door in no time.

After inspecting the situation, the midwife announced that

there was no time to get my wife to hospital; it would have to be a home delivery! Mrs King then told us that she had promised Angela, a young trainee midwife, that she could deliver the baby. She rang her on the telephone, and then announced that she was going to collect her from Shoeburyness, two miles away! Whether it was fear on my part, or generosity, (I suspect the former!) I promptly offered to go and collect the young midwife. I left immediately and drove quite speedily there and back.

Angela went into the house, while I parked the car. Two minutes later, as I stepped into the bedroom, the baby cried! While I took in the news that it was another daughter, it dawned on me, as I stood back out of the way of the two midwives, that, if I had not called Mrs King, or she had gone to collect the young midwife, I would have delivered the baby!

A little later Mrs King asked, 'Where's the baby's cot?' My wife was quite alert enough to drop me in it; 'He hasn't got it down from the loft', she informed the midwives. 'No problem', Mrs King replied. She pulled a drawer from a white chest of drawers and asked, 'Where can I tip these clothes?' Then, 'Have you got a soft towel?' Our new baby was laid gently in the make-shift cot and so slept her first night, and some of her first day, in a drawer! (Not returned to its place!)

We decided to name our new baby girl Angela, after the young midwife who just managed to deliver her.

Joseph, Mary's husband, would seem to have been faced with a very similar situation. We have no information about what actually happened, but presumably he had to deliver, or help to deliver, the baby. There was no cot available, so the animals' eating trough, a manger, had to be used instead. However, the spotlight, in this the fourth week of Advent, is not upon Joseph but upon his wife, Miriam (the name in Hebrew), whom we know as 'Mary' (from the Greek, *Mariae* and the Latin *Maria*).

From the Gospels we know very little about Mary of Nazareth. We are not even sure of her parents' names, although there is a long tradition that they were called Joachim and Anne. An apocryphal book, called *The Gospel of the Birth of Mary,* appeared in the Middle Ages, purporting to tell the story of how Mary was born of Anne and Joachim. The writer appears to have taken his material from several sources, including a book called *The Book of James,* or *The Protevangelium,* which is dated from the middle of the second century (the Gospels accepted as authentic by the Church were written some seventy years before). It is a mishmash of legend and novelistic folklore and totally unreliable as a source.

What impressed the very earliest, reliable, Christian writers (for example, Justin Martyr d.165 and Irenaeus d.202) was Mary's obedience to God; they contrast this with the dis-obedience of Eve.

What is also impressive is her faith and trust in God. It is generally believed by the Biblical scholars that Mary was almost certainly 12 or 13 years of age when she was asked by God to be the mother of the Messiah. She was probably only 13, then, when she had Jesus. What a responsibility for a girl of her age!

Some years ago, when I was caught up in Youth Work and deeply immersed in the problems of teenagers, I went to a wedding reception of a friend. During the course of the evening, I stood at the back of the hall, drink in hand, talking to a tall, fit-looking, older man, who proudly told me that he was in his eighties. The conversation got round to 'young people today'. Stan expressed the opinion that they did not have sufficient responsibility early enough in their lives; they were kept as children far too long. He illustrated his views with the following information. He had left school at 14, like everyone else in those days, and, living at Greenwich, had started work on the Thames barges. By 15 years of age, he told me, he was solely responsible for 'rowing' (this meant *steering*) a large laden barge up and down the commercial length of the Thames. With pride in his voice, Stan described how he did this, in the dark and the river fog, by knowing the sounds of the river. 'You went up with the tide and down with the tide; in all weathers, he said. At 16 he was awarded the freedom of the river, when he officially became a Lighterman.

Stan may well have a valuable point; young people today are so often spoon-fed and cosseted. Giving them real responsibility much earlier in life might help some of them mature earlier and act more responsibly. Certainly young people like Mary of Nazareth, of first century Palestine, had to take on heavy responsibilities at, what would appear to us, a very early age.

The whole story of how God chose to become a human being, is totally amazing. The infinite, all-powerful, all-knowing Spirit, who holds in existence the immeasurable universe of a billion galaxies, galaxies that are 400 million light-years apart, asked a 13-year-old Jewish peasant girl if she would consider being the human mother of the Godhead! And God waited for a reply. Mary had been assured, at the beginning of the request, not to worry; 'Do not be afraid' the messenger said. Then, after a down-to earth question about how it was going to be possible, since she was a virgin, Mary said, 'Let what you have said be done to me'; in other words, God received the 'yes' he was waiting and hoping for! The infinite Creator respects human freedom.

Students have sometimes asked me, 'What if Mary had said "no"?' The first point, in an answer, would be; God would not act against her wishes, nor would he force her to do what he wanted. God knew the sort of person Mary was, so her reply was in keeping with her generous nature.

With her faith in God, her 'yes' to him, Mary takes on an incredible responsibility. She could not have understood the full implications of what had just taken place within her. How could she have known that, by her acceptance of the will of God, she was destined to be the most important and most famous woman in the whole of human history? It is a wonderfully simple, and inspiring, example of abandoning oneself, with complete trust, into the loving hands of the Father of all.

After receiving the message from God, Mary must have been confused and bewildered. She must have begun to wonder whether she had dreamed it; *surely not me*, you can imagine her saying to herself. But she had been left with a sign; she could check that out. If her aunt, Elizabeth, who was childless and past the usual time for having a family, was really pregnant, then she, Mary, could rely upon what she had heard. As Luke's Gospel says, 'Mary got ready and *hurried* to a town in the hill country of Judea'. And, sure enough, Elizabeth was six months pregnant!

A few years ago I caused a furore by writing a letter to the *Daily Mail*, pointing out an error in an account of the Nativity story that they had published and drawing readers' attention to the fact that neither Luke nor Matthew make any mention of Mary riding a donkey to Bethlehem. I suppose that I made matters worse by adding that *if* there had been a donkey, which was very unlikely as they were a poor couple, then, in those sexist times, Joseph would have ridden the animal and Mary would have walked behind! I even received a letter from my Bishop informing me that he had received complaints. In an exchange of correspondence between us, he accepted what I had tried to do. This was to turn people's attention away from the emotional and romantic traditions of Christmas; to look at what the Gospels really tell us and get beneath the surface to the meaning of it all. It is shallow and superficial to worry about whether there was or was not a donkey and who rode it. The real truth, what the event really means, is too stupendous and awe-inspiring to waste time on inconsequential detail. The poet Sir John Betjeman (1906-1984) in his Christmas poem, which begins with the words, *The bells of waiting Advent ring*, tried to capture the awe of it:

And is it true? And is it true,
This most tremendous tale of all,
Seen in a stained-glass window's hue
A Baby in an ox's stall?
The maker of the stars and sea
Become a Child on earth for me?

And is it true? For if it is,
No loving fingers tying strings
Around those tissued fripperies,
The sweet and silly Christmas things,
Bath salts and inexpensive scent
And hideous tie so kindly meant,
No love that in a family dwells,
No carolling in frosty air,
Nor all the steeple-shaking bells
Can with this single Truth compare –
That God was Man in Palestine
And lives today in Bread and Wine.

Another famous poet, Christina Rossetti (1830-1894), summed up the whole awesome truth, simply and beautifully, with the words, 'Love came down at Christmas'. St John expressed it, more theologically, in his Gospel, with the well-known phrase 'the Word was made flesh and dwelt among us' (John 1:14). This is the belief that we know as the Incarnation.

There is so much to meditate upon in this the fourth week of Advent. We have already considered Christ coming, one day, as our judge; preparing for the coming of Christ as our teacher, by repentance; Christ among us today and always as our guide. Now we have before us the deep and inspiring faith of Mary and, even harder to take in, the astounding trust of our Creator God, who placed himself in the care of a simple 13-year-old girl as a totally helpless baby! No human words are adequate to express the wonder of this.

If we are serious about advancing in our prayer-life, what is often called, the spiritual life, we need to adopt the approach of Mary, the Mother of the Lord. She placed herself totally in God's hands; abandoned herself to him in complete trust. The prayer below (at the end of the session) is the prayer of Charles de Foucauld, a French missionary and mystic; it could so easily be the prayer of Mary, after her acceptance of God's destiny for her.

Summary

In a family the preparations for the arrival of a new baby are important; Mary and Joseph were materially poorly prepared. The very young Mary accepted the most responsible role ever asked of a woman; God had to wait upon her answer! In this we see God respecting human freedom. Mary confirmed the truth of her experience by visiting her pregnant aunt, Elizabeth.

We trivialise Christmas so easily and constantly need to remind ourselves of its true meaning. The Creator of the Universe chose to become a weak and helpless human baby in the care of a poor peasant couple. Love came down at Christmas.

Bible reading

Luke 1:26-38
(Alternatives Luke 1:39-45 or Matthew 1:18-25)

Discussion points

1. Has any member of the group any 'birth' experiences to share? (*Briefly*)

2. Did the above text present any surprises? For example, how young Mary was when she had Jesus?

3. Which do you think is the most surprising and impressive; that God waited on Mary's reply before proceeding with his plan, or that God entrusted his Son to a poor peasant family?

4. Do the words 'Love came down at Christmas' cry out for a response? If so, what sort of response?

5. There are so many jobs to be done in preparation for Christmas; what *spiritual* preparation might we make, springing from this course?

6. Has this course revealed a need for a better understanding of Scripture? How could this be remedied?

7. Would the group benefit from some sort of mutual support, for example, more time together, perhaps during Lent?

Prayer

Father,
I abandon myself into your hands;
do with me what you will.
Whatever you may do I thank you:
I am ready for all, I accept all.

Let only your will be done in me,
and all your creatures.
I wish no more than this, O Lord.

Into your hands I commend my soul:
I offer it to you
with all the love of my heart,
for I love you, Lord,
and so need to give myself,
to surrender myself into your hands,
without reserve,
and with boundless confidence,
for you are my Father.
Amen.

Charles de Foucauld

Acknowledgements

The author and publishers wish to express their gratitude to the following for permission to include copyright material in this publication:

John Murray (Publishers) Ltd, 50 Albemarle Street, London W1X 4BD for the extract from Sir John Betjeman's Christmas poem *The Bells of Waiting Advent Ring*.

Solo Syndication Ltd, 49-53 Kensington High Street, London W8 5ED for the extract from *The Daily Mail* dated 20 December 1997.

Orbis Books, Mary Knoll, NY 10545, USA for the quotation by Oscar Romero, 'Advent should admonish us to discover . . .'

The Abbot of the Stravropegic Monastery of St John the Baptist, Maldon, Essex for an extract from *We shall see Him as He is* by Archimandrite Sophrony, 1988.

The Poor Servants of the Mother of God of 'Maryfield', Roehampton, London SW15 for the prayer of their foundress, Mother Magdalen Taylor.